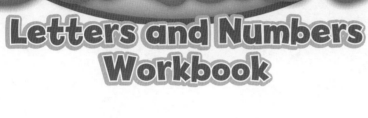

Super Safari 2

Letters and Numbers
Workbook

Color in Leo!

 CAMBRIDGE
UNIVERSITY PRESS

Shaftesbury Road, Cambridge CB2 8EA, United Kingdom

One Liberty Plaza, 20th Floor, New York, NY 10006, USA

477 Williamstown Road, Port Melbourne, VIC 3207, Australia

314–321, 3rd Floor, Plot 3, Splendor Forum, Jasola District Centre, New Delhi – 110025, India

103 Penang Road, #05–06/07, Visioncrest Commercial, Singapore 238467

Torre de los Parques, Colonia Tlacoquemécatl del Valle, Mexico City CP 03200, Mexico

Cambridge University Press & Assessment is a department of the University of Cambridge.

We share the University's mission to contribute to society through the pursuit of education, learning and research at the highest international levels of excellence.

First published 2016

20 19 18 17 16 15 14 13 12 11

Printed in Poland by Opolgraf

ISBN 978-1-316-60951-4 Letters and Numbers Workbook 2

Additional resources for this publication at www.cambridge.org/supersafari

Cambridge University Press has no responsibility for the persistence or accuracy of URLs for external or third-party internet websites referred to in this publication, and does not guarantee that any content on such websites is, or will remain, accurate or appropriate. Information regarding prices, travel timetables, and other factual information given in this work is correct at the time of first printing but Cambridge University Press does not guarantee the accuracy of such information thereafter.

Super Safari 2

Letters and Numbers Workbook

Hello!

1 **Draw and trace.**

I'm _____ .

1 **Trace and color.**

The children point to the numbers and name them. Then they count the objects aloud. Finally, the children trace over the dotted lines from the numbers to the objects.

1

2

3

1 My school

Present the letter. The children trace and write the letters with different colored crayons. Finally, the children color the apple freely.

1 Trace and write. Color the picture.

1 **Count and trace. Color the objects.**

Present the numbers. The children identify the objects and count them. Then they trace the numbers with different colored crayons. Finally, the children color the objects freely.

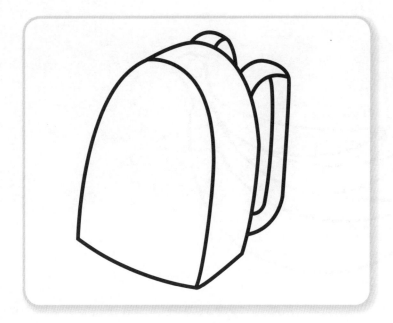

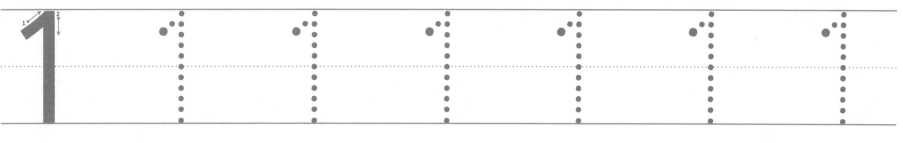

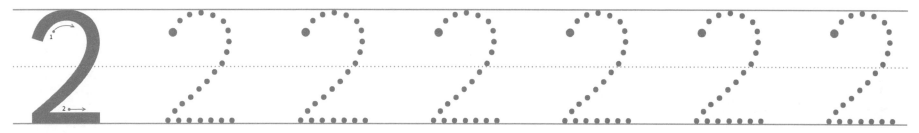

1 **Trace and write. Finger-paint.**

Present the letter. Then the children trace and write the letters with different colored crayons. Finally, the children finger-paint the banana.

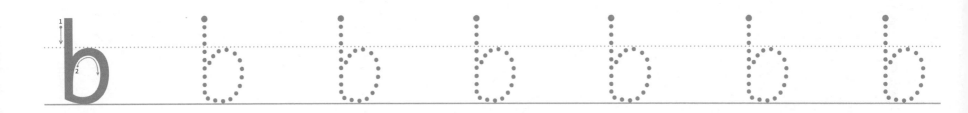

1 **Count and trace. Color the objects.**

Present the numbers. The children trace a line from the number 3 to the crayons. Continue in the same manner with the number 4. Finally, the children trace the numbers with colored crayons.

3 - - - - - - - - - - - - - - -

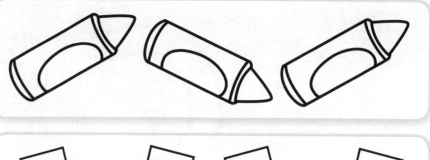

4 - - - - - - - - - - - - - - -

3 3 3 3 3 3

4 4 4 4 4 4

1 **Trace and write. Color the pictures.**

Present the letter. Then the children trace and write the letters with different colored crayons. Finally, the children color the cow and letter freely.

C c c c c c c

C

1 Count and color. Trace the numbers.

Present the numbers. The children count the computers and color them. Then they trace the number 5. Repeat the procedure for the boards and the number 6.

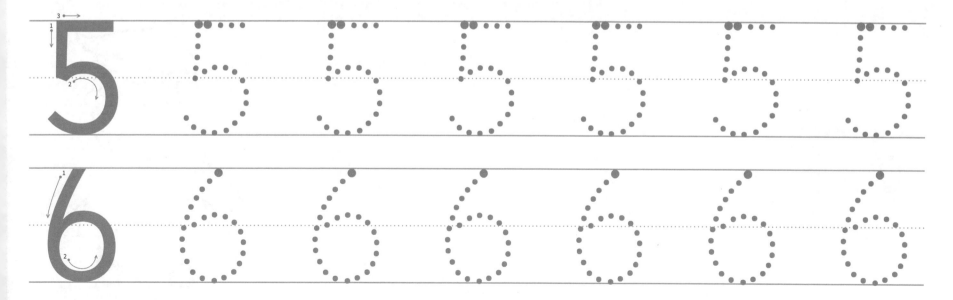

1 **Trace and color.**

Ask the children to point to letter "a" and say /æ/ – /æ/ – /æ/ – *cat*. Ask the children to find the letter "a" in the word *cat*. Then the children trace the dotted lines from letter "a" to the pictures. Repeat the procedure with *dad*. Finally, the children color the pictures freely.

c<u>**a**</u>**t**

d<u>**a**</u>**d**

1 Color the objects. Cut and glue.

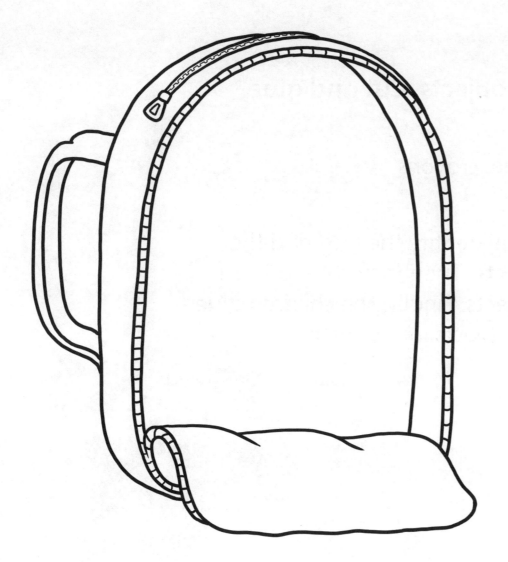

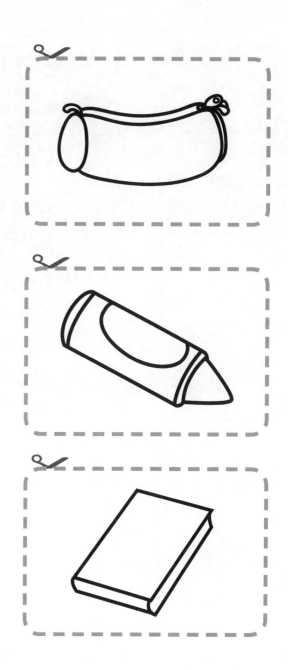

Color the objects. Cut and glue.

Materials:
scissors, glue, crayons

Instructions:
The children identify the bag and the school objects. Then they color and cut out the objects. Finally, the children glue the school objects inside the bag.

1 Look and color.

The children point to the desk on the left side of the page. Then they find the other desk in the row. The children color the desk. Continue in the same manner with the pencil case and the sheet of paper.

Present the letter. The children color the pictures for the words that start with the letter "d". The children trace and write the letters with different colored crayons.

1 Color the pictures. Trace and write.

dinosaur

dog

apple

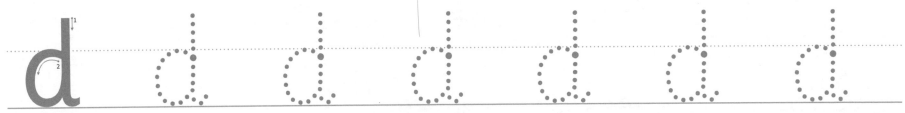

d

1 **Count and trace. Color the objects.**

Present the numbers. The children count the circles in each number and color them. Then the children trace the numbers with different colored crayons.

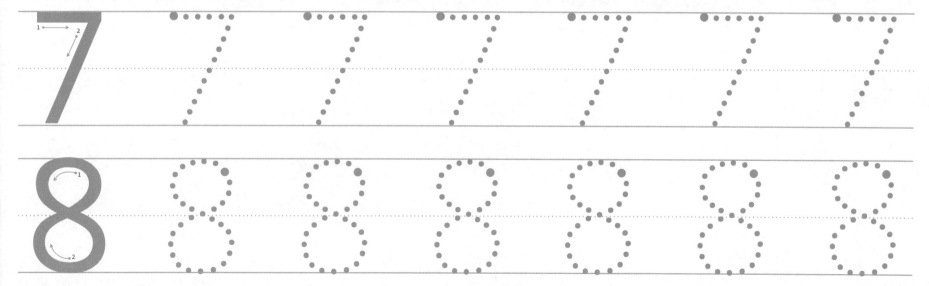

1 **Color the letters. Trace and write.**

Present the letter. The children look at the letters in the box and color the letters "e". Then the children trace and write the letters with different colored crayons.

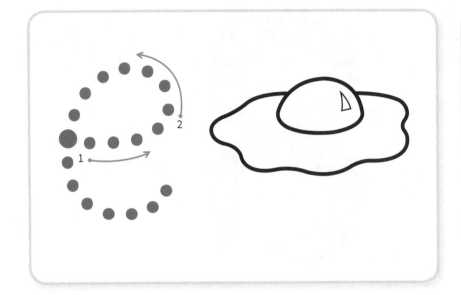

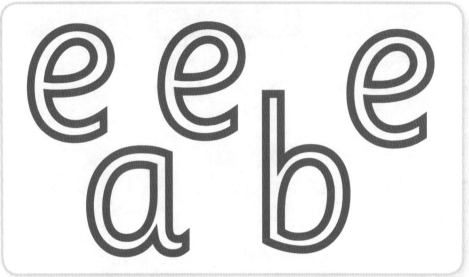

1 Draw, trace and write.

Present the number. Then the children draw the corresponding number of balls inside each box. The children trace the numbers with different colored crayons.

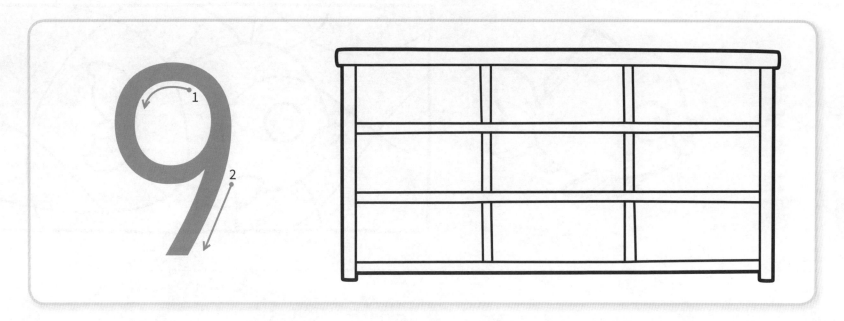

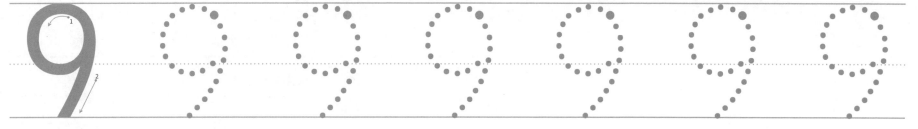

1 **Find and color the fish. Trace and write.**

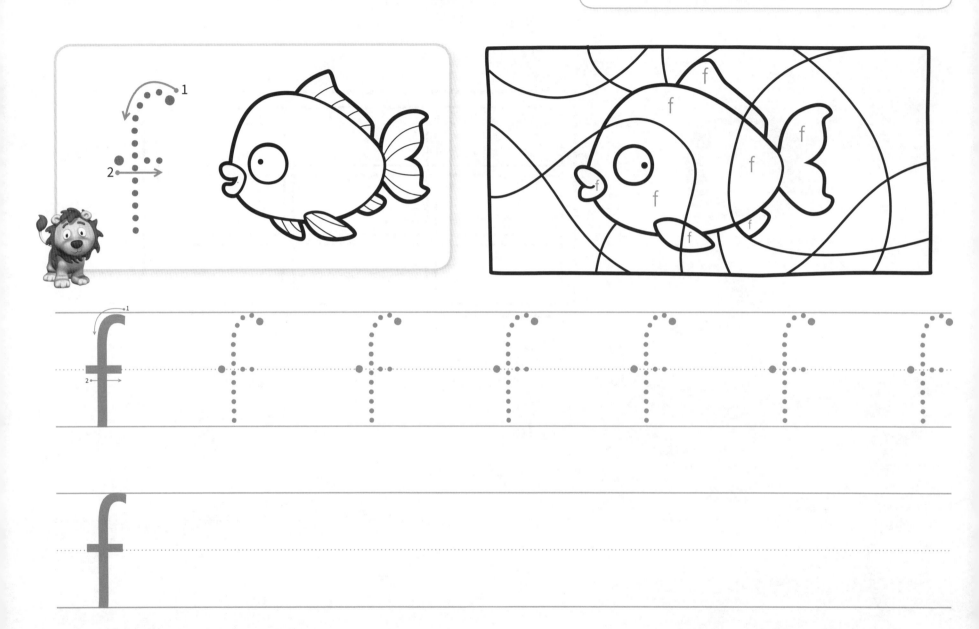

1 **Count and color the fingers. Trace.**

Present the number. Then the children count and color the fingers. Finally, the children trace and write the numbers with different colored crayons.

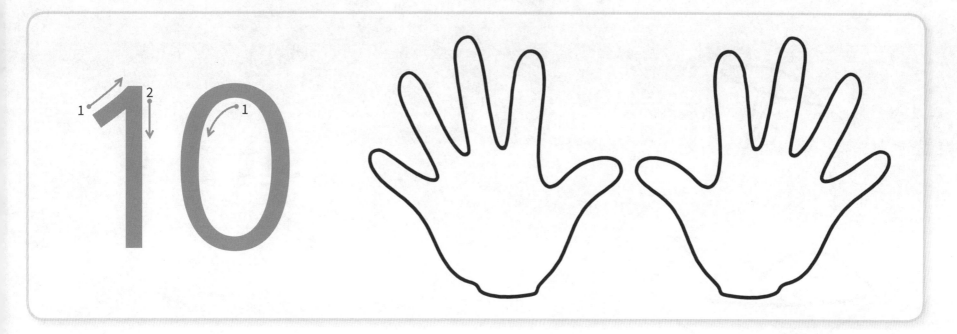

10　10　10　10　10　10　10　10　10　10

10

1 **Trace and color.**

Ask the children to point to the first picture and say /ɪ/ – /ɪ/ – /ɪ/ – pin. Repeat the procedure with lip and sit. The children match the pictures to the words. Finally, they color the pictures.

s_it

p_in

l_ip

1 Color, cut, and assemble.

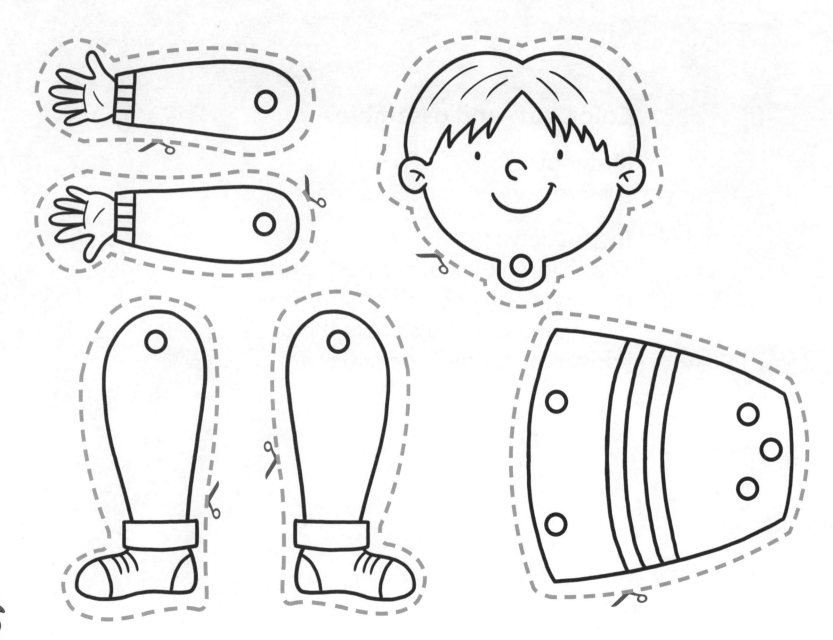

Color, cut, and assemble.

Materials:

scissors, crayons, paper fastener clips

Instructions:

The children look at the body parts, identify them, and color them. Then they cut them out and assemble the boy's body using paper fastener clips.

1 Match the body parts.

The children trace a line from the left hand to the right hand with their fingers first. Continue in the same manner with the rest of the body parts. Then the children trace lines with different colored crayons.

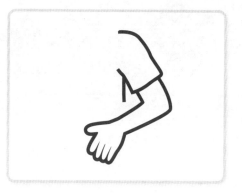

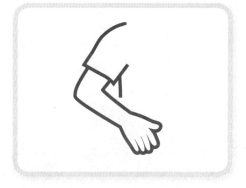

3 My room

1 Trace and write. Color the picture.

g g g g g g

g

1 **Count and color the pictures. Trace.**

1 **Trace and write. Finger-paint.**

Present the letter. The children trace and write the letters with different colored crayons. Next, they dip their fingers in yellow finger paint and print their fingerprints along the letter "h" and the hat.

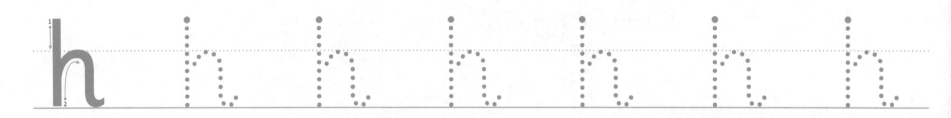

1 **Count and color the pictures. Trace.**

Present the number. Then the children count the dolls and color them freely. Finally, the children trace the numbers with different colored crayons.

1 **Color the letter and the picture. Trace and write.**

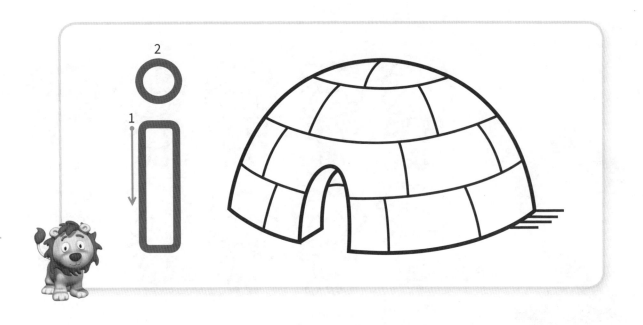

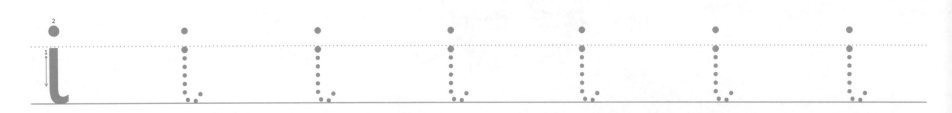

1 **Count and circle. Trace. Color the pictures.**

The children count the dolls and circle the corresponding number. Repeat the same procedure for the puzzles. Then the children trace the numbers with different colored crayons. Finally, the children color the pictures freely.

11 / 12

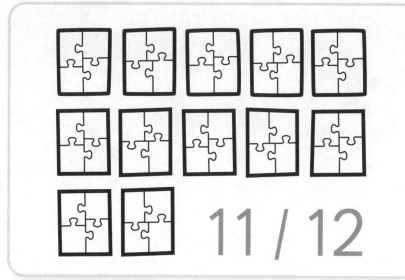

11 / 12

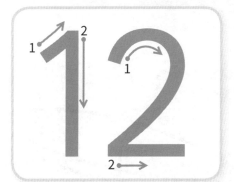

1 **Trace. Color the pictures.**

The children point to letter "e" and say /e/ – /e/ – /e/ – *bed*. Then they find the letter "e" in the word *bed*. Next, the children trace the dotted lines from the letter "e" to the picture. Repeat the procedure for the word *pen*. Finally, the children color the pictures freely.

e

b<u>e</u>d

e

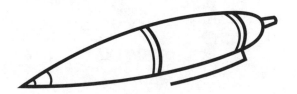

p<u>e</u>n

1 **Paint the box. Color the toys. Cut out and assemble.**

Paint the box. Color the toys. Cut out and assemble.

Materials:
scissors, paint, brushes, crayons, glue

Instructions:
The children paint the toy box. Then they color the toys with colored crayons. Next, they cut out the strips and make two slots in the toy box. Help the children insert the strip through the slots and pull on it from side to side to move the figures. Finally, the children name the toys in the toy box.

1 **Listen and draw.**

Say *Point to the toy box.* The children follow the instruction. Draw a ball in a toy box on the board. Ask *Where is the ball? In the toy box. Draw a ball in the toy box.* Repeat the procedure with *Draw a book under the table.*

4 In the jungle

Present the letter. Then the children color the pictures of the words that start with the letter "j". Finally, the children trace and write the letters with different colored crayons.

1 Color the pictures. Trace and write.

jacket

<u>h</u>at

jet

J

j

1 **Count and color the pictures. Trace.**

Present the number. The children count the snakes and color them freely. Finally, they trace the numbers with different colored crayons.

1 **Color the letters. Trace and write.**

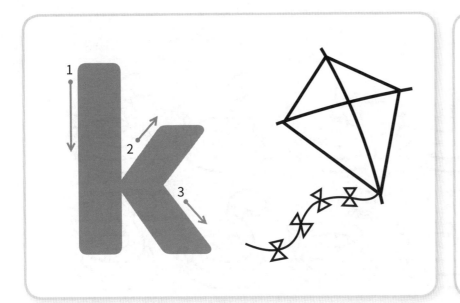

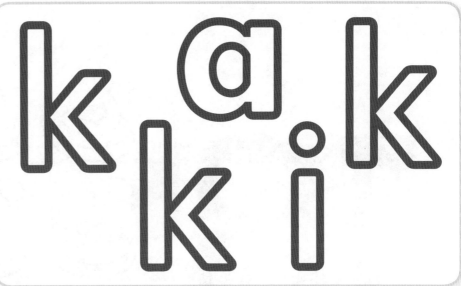

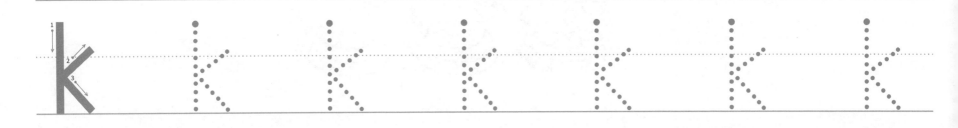

1 **Count and color the pictures. Trace.**

Present the number. Then the children count the tigers and color them freely. Finally, they trace the numbers with different colored crayons.

1 Find and color the lion. Trace and write.

Present the letter. The children find the letters "l" in the picture and color the corresponding sections. Finally, they trace and write the letters with different colored crayons.

1 **Count and color the pictures. Trace.**

Review the numbers. Then the children count the fish and the cats and color them freely. Finally, they trace the numbers with different colored crayons.

13

14

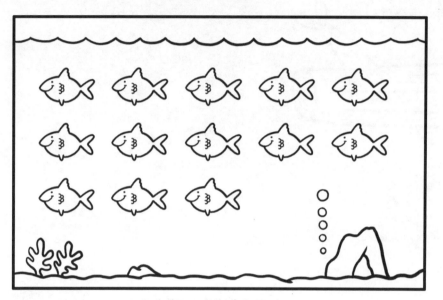

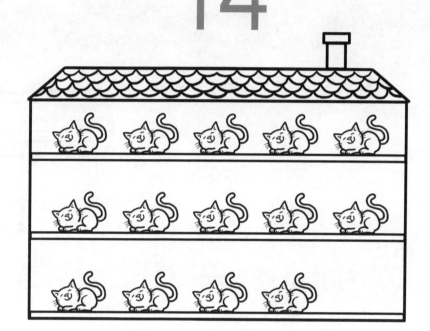

13   13   13   13   13   13

14   14   14   14   14   14

1 **Listen and circle. Color the pictures.**

Write the word *log*. The children say /ɒ/ – /ɒ/ – /ɒ/ – *log*. Repeat the procedure with *dot* and *pot*. Next, the children circle the correct word for each picture. Finally, they color the pictures freely.

l**o**g

p**o**t / d**o**t

d**o**t / p**o**t

1 Match, glue, and color.

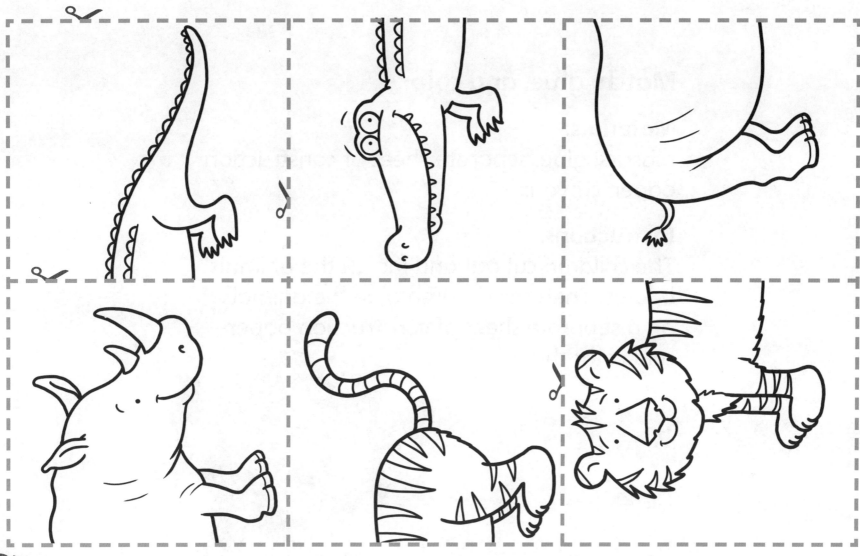

Match, glue, and color.

Materials:
scissors, glue, separate sheet of construction paper, crayons

Instructions:
The children cut out and match the animals' bodies. Then the children glue the animals on a separate sheet of construction paper and color them.

1 Look and match.

Show the children how to match the close up of the crocodile with the full picture of the animal. Repeat the procedure for the rest of the shapes and animals.

5 Fruits and vegetables

1 **Color the picture. Trace and write.**

Present the letter. Then the children color the mouse freely.
Finally, they trace and write the letters with different colored crayons.

m

1 **Follow and draw.**

Review the numbers. Then the children follow the lines from the picture to the number, and finally to the box. The children draw the corresponding number of food items in the box.

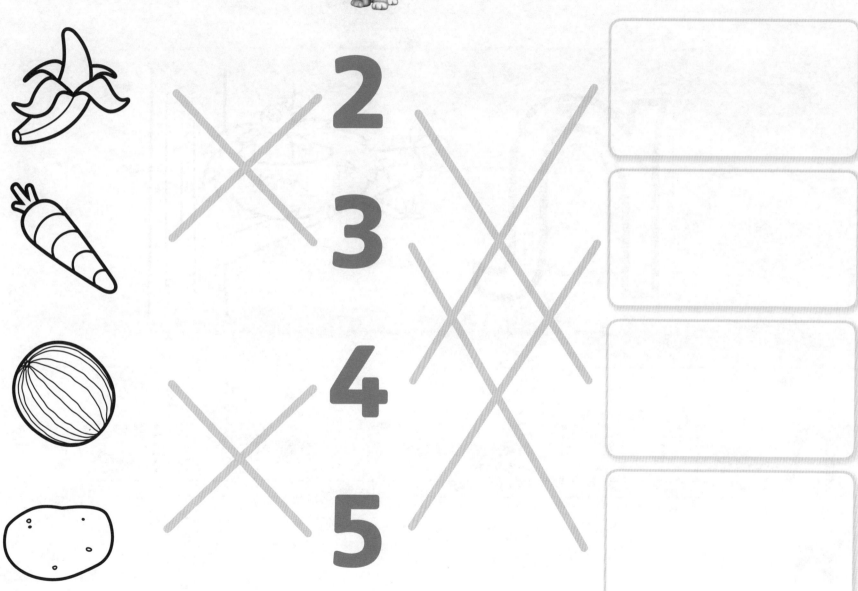

1 **Finger-paint. Trace and write.**

Present the letter. The children dip their fingers in finger paint and print their fingerprints along the letter "n" and the nest. Finally, the children trace and write the letters with different colored crayons.

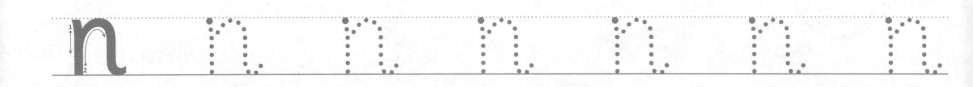

n

1 Count and circle.

Review the numbers from 1 to 10. The children look at the pictures of the tomatoes. They count the tomatoes aloud and circle the corresponding number. Repeat the procedure for the remaining food items.

6 / 7

8 / 7

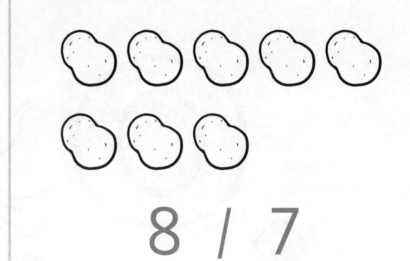

9 / 7

10 / 9

1 **Color the letter and the picture. Trace and write.**

Present the letter. The children color the letter "o" and the octopus freely. Finally, the children trace and write the letters with different colored crayons.

1 **Trace the numbers. Draw.**

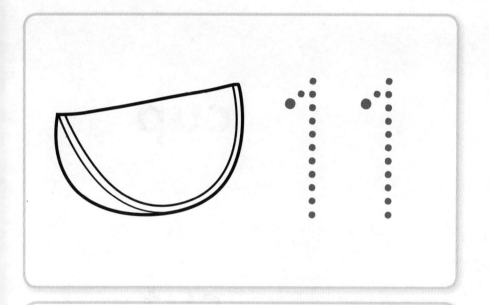

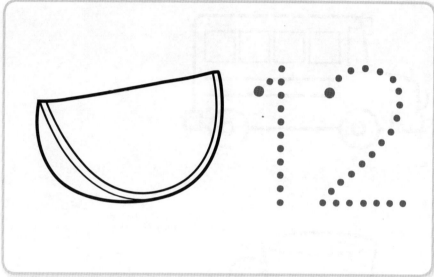

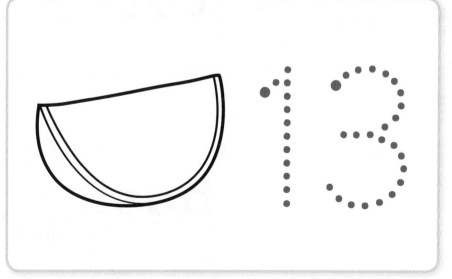

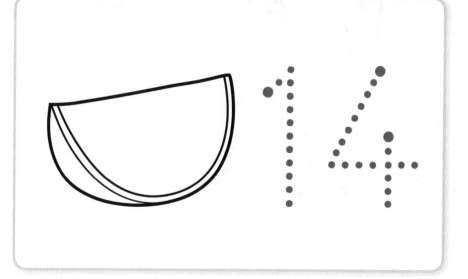

1 **Follow the maze and trace.**

Ask the children to point to the first picture and say /ʌ/ – /ʌ/ – /ʌ/ – *bus*. The children copy. The children trace the lines from the picture to the word. The children find the letter "u" in in each word. Finally, they color the pictures freely.

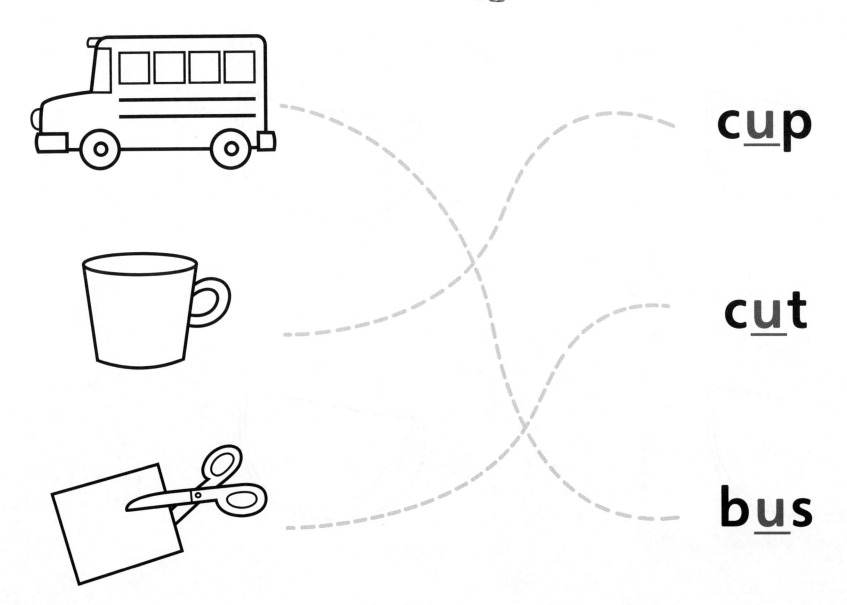

c<u>u</u>p

c<u>u</u>t

b<u>u</u>s

1 Color, cut, and assemble.

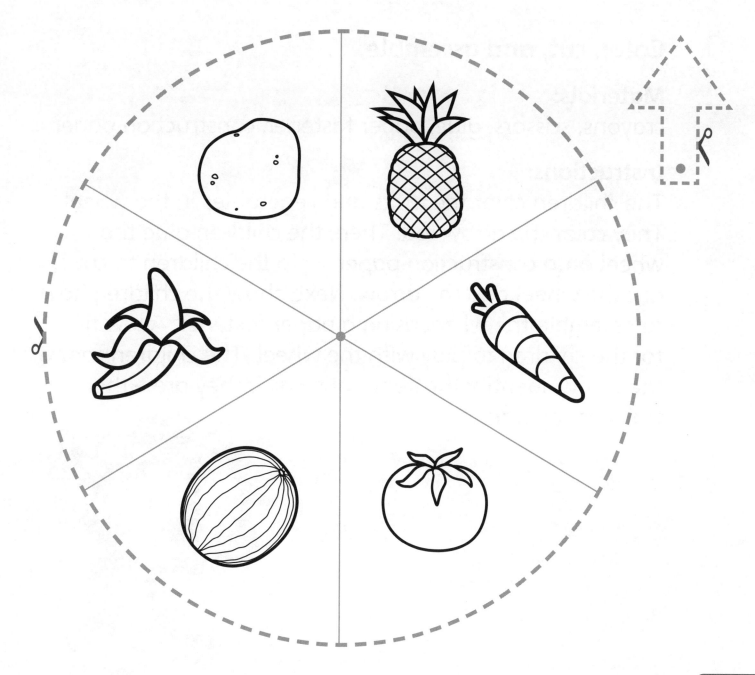

Color, cut, and assemble.

Materials:
crayons, scissors, glue, paper fastener, construction paper

Instructions:
The children color the fruits and vegetables in the wheel. They color the arrow red. Then, the children glue the wheel onto construction paper. Help the children to cut out the wheel and the arrow. Next, show the children how to assemble the wheel using a paper fastener. Allow time for the children to play with the wheel. The children spin the arrow, identify the items, and say if they are either fruits or vegetables.

1 **Listen and color the pictures.**

The children color the fruits and vegetables with different colored crayons according to your instructions: pineapple – yellow, watermelon – green, tomato – red, and carrot – orange.

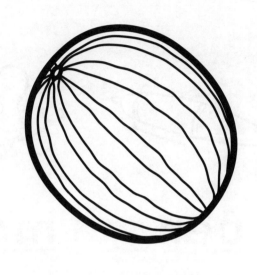

6 My town

Present the letter. The children color the pictures of the words that start with the letter "p". Finally, the children trace and write the letters with different colored crayons.

1 **Color the pictures. Trace and write.**

pen **mouse** **puppy**

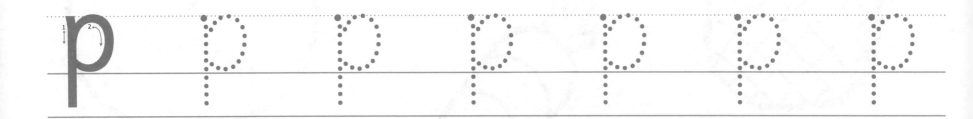

1 **Count and color the pictures. Trace.**

1 Color the letters. Trace and write.

Present the letter. The children identify the letters "q" and color them. Then the children color in the picture. Finally, they trace and write the letters with different colored crayons.

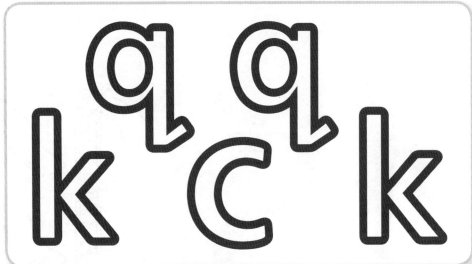

1 **Count and color the pictures. Trace.**

Present the number. Then children count the robots and color them freely. Finally, the children trace the numbers with different colored crayons.

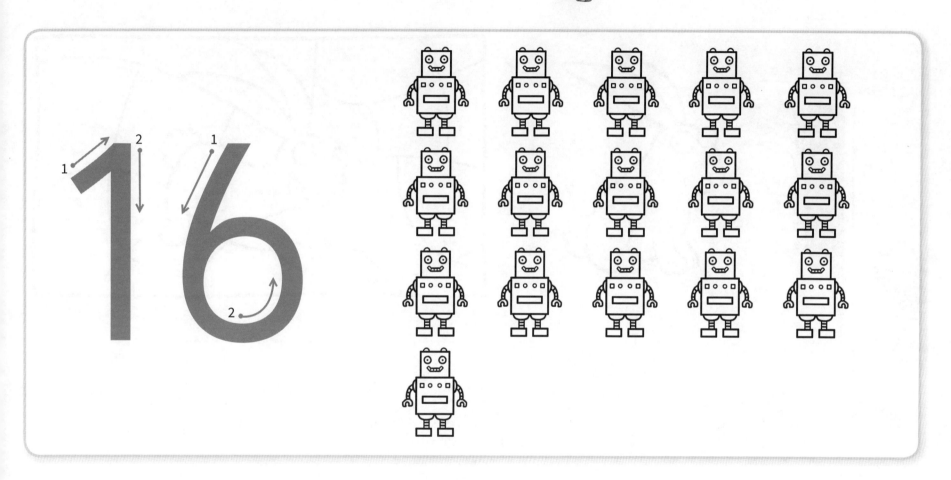

1 **Find and color the rabbit. Trace and write.**

Present the letter. The children find the letters "r" in the picture and color the corresponding sections. Finally, the children trace and write the letters with different colored crayons.

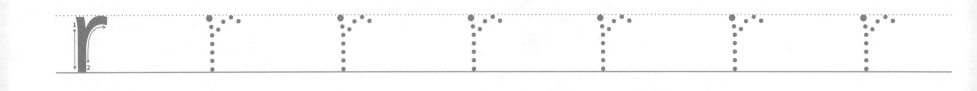

1 **Count and draw one more. Trace.**

Review the numbers. The children count the round presents and draw one more to complete 15. Repeat the procedure for the square presents. Finally, the children trace the numbers with different colored crayons.

15

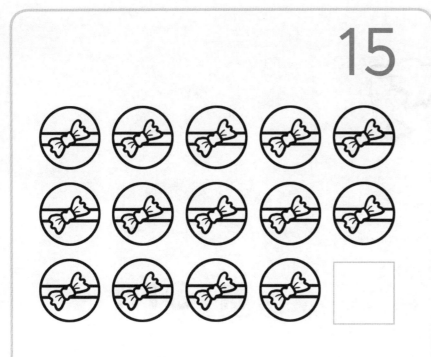

16

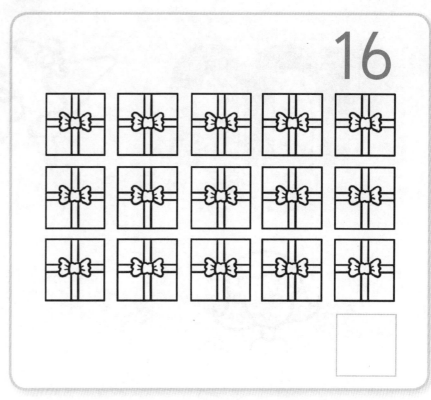

15 15 15 15 15 15 15

16 16 16 16 16 16 16

1 **Look and match.**

The children point to the map. Say /m/ – /m/ – /m/ – *map*. Continue in the same manner with *mom*, *mop*, and *marker*. The children identify the pictures on the left and draw lines to match them with the corresponding pictures on the right.

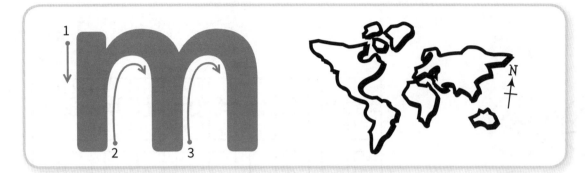

mom

mop

marker

1 Make a model.

PARK

SCHOOL

TOY STORE

SUPERMARKET

ZOO

BUS STOP

Make a model.

Materials:
waterpaints, paintbrush, construction paper, scissors, tape, glue

Preparation:
Cut out small right-angled triangles (5 cm tall) out of construction paper.

Instructions:
The children name the places. The children paint the pictures. Then the children glue the paper onto a piece of construction paper. Help the children cut out the strips.
Then help the children attach the triangles to the back of the strips with tape, so the buildings can stand up to form streets.

1 **Look and trace the path. Color the picture.**

Ask the children where the boy and girl in the picture are. The children follow the path to the swing. Then the children go to the slide, then to the seesaw, and lastly to the merry-go-round. Finally, the children trace the path and color the playground equipment freely.

Present the letter. The children trace and write the letters with different colored crayons. Finally, the children color the sun freely.

1 Trace and write. Color the picture.

S S S S S S S S

S

1 **Count and color the pictures. Trace.**

1 **Finger-paint. Trace and write.**

Present the letter. The children dip their fingers in finger paint and print them along the letter "t" and the table. Finally, the children trace and write the letters with different colored crayons.

1 **Count and color the pictures. Trace.**

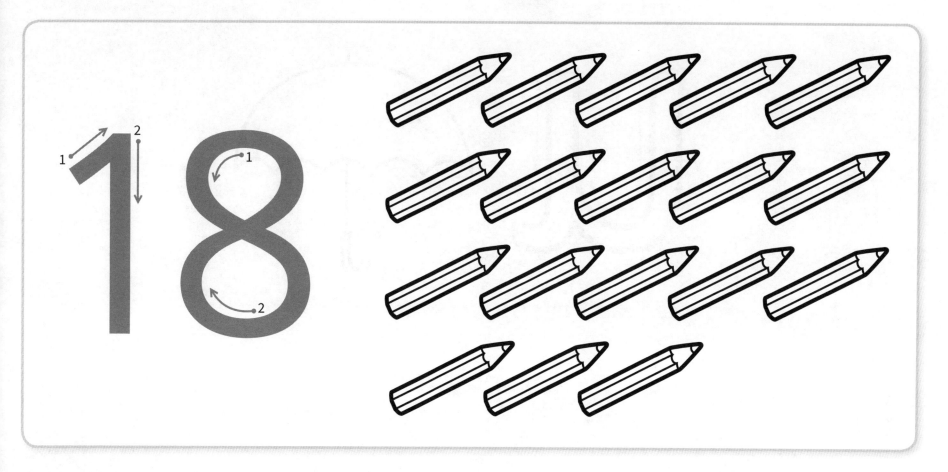

1 **Color the letter and the picture. Trace and write.**

Present the letter. The children color the letter "u" and the umbrella freely. Finally, the children trace and write the letters with different colored crayons.

1 Trace. Count and color the pictures.

Review the numbers. The children trace the numbers with different colored crayons. Next, the children count the firefighter helmets and write the corresponding number on the lines. Repeat the procedure for the other helmets. Finally, the children color all the helmets freely.

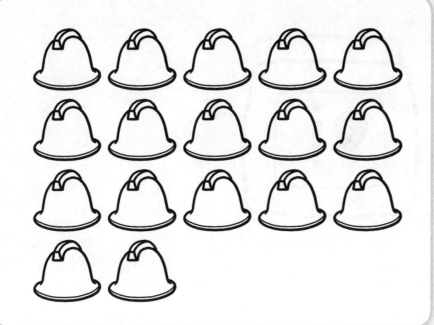

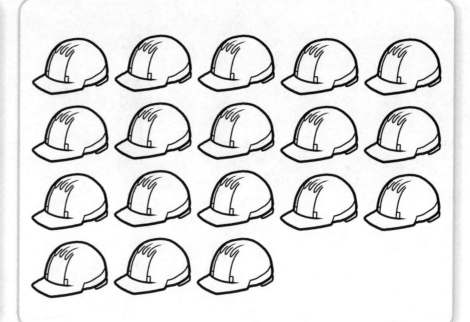

17 17 17 17 17 17 17 17

18 18 18 18 18 18 18 18

1 Listen and color the pictures.

The children point to the jar. Say /dʒ/ – /dʒ/ – /dʒ/ – jar.
Say *Color the picture that is the same.* Say *Listen /dʒ/ – jet; /m/ – map?*
Are they the same? No. Continue in the same manner with the rest of the activity. The children color the picture that is the same. Repeat the procedure for the rest of the activity.

 jet

 jeans

  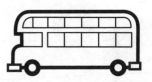

1 Make stick puppets. Role-play.

Make stick puppets. Role-play.

Materials:
construction paper, scissors, glue, colored crayons, craft sticks

Instructions:
The children look at the community workers and color them freely. Then the children glue the workers onto a piece of construction paper. Once dry, the children cut out the workers. Next, the children glue a craft stick at the back of each cutout. Let dry. Finally, the children use their puppets to role-play: *I am a firefighter.*

1 **Look and match.**

Say *firefighter*. The children repeat. Continue in the same manner with *teacher*, *farmer*, and *doctor*. Then the children match the workplaces with the corresponding workers. Then say *This is a hose. Who uses a hose? The firefighter*. Continue in the same manner with the rest of the activity. Finally, the children match the workers with the items they use.

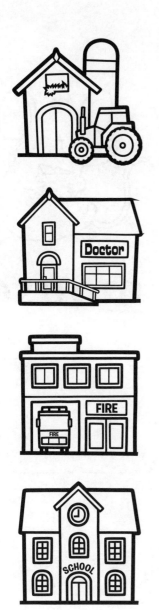

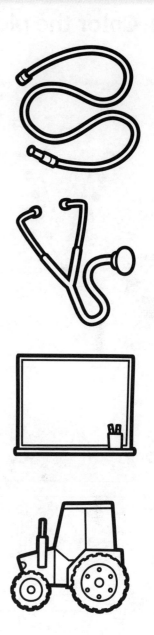

Present the letter. The children color the pictures of the words that start with letter "v". Finally, the children trace and write the letters with different colored crayons.

1 Color the pictures. Trace and write.

<u>v</u>est

<u>v</u>an

<u>m</u>ouse

V v v v v v v

V

1 **Count and color the pictures. Trace.**

1 **Color the letters. Trace and write.**

Present the letter. The children identify and color the letters "w" in the box. Finally, they trace and write the letters with different colored crayons.

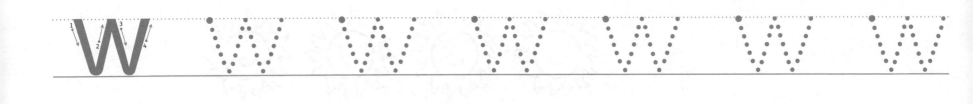

1 **Count and color the pictures. Trace.**

Present the number. The children count the flowers and color them freely. Finally, the children trace the numbers with different colored crayons.

1 **Trace and write. Color the picture.**

Present the letter. The children trace and write the letters with different colored crayons. Finally, the children color the picture freely.

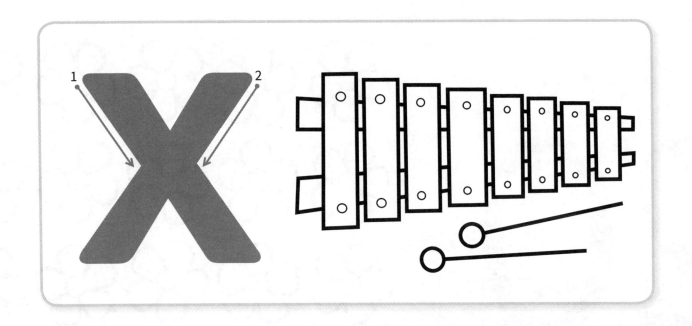

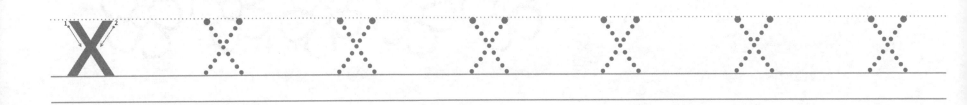

1 **Look and draw. Trace the numbers.**

Review the numbers. Then the children identify the number 19 and draw the corresponding number of snowflakes. Repeat the procedure for the number 20 and the flowers. Finally, the children trace the numbers with different colored crayons.

19

20

19   19   19   19   19   19   19

20   20   20   20   20   20   20

1 **Listen and trace. Color the pictures.**

The children point to the log. Say /l/ – /l/ – /l/ – *log*. Continue in the same manner with *lamp* and *lion*. The children identify the pictures in the left column and trace the dotted lines to match the pictures to the words. Finally, the children color the pictures freely.

log

lamp

lion

1 **Make a mobile.**

Make a mobile.

Materials:
colored crayons, construction paper, scissors, cotton balls, glue, plastic clothes hanger, knotted thread of different lengths, hole punch

Preparation:
Make small cotton balls and distribute them among children. Cut knotted threads of different lengths (3 per child)

Instructions:
The children cut out the sun and the clouds and glue them onto a piece of construction paper. Then they color the sun and glue the cotton balls onto the clouds. Once dry, the children cut out the sun and the clouds. Make a hole at the top of each item with a hole punch. Help the children pull a string through each hole and tie the sun and the clouds to their clothes hanger.

1 **Look and color the pictures.**

Ask *What's the weather like?* The children identify the two kinds of weather: *sunny* and *snowy*. Then the children color the objects that correspond to each type of weather.

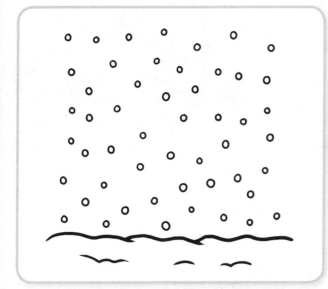

Present the letter. The children trace and write the letters on the lines. Finally, the children color the picture freely.

1 Trace and write. Color the picture.

1 **Draw one more and match. Color the pictures.**

Review the numbers from 1 to 10. Then the children draw one object in each box. Next, the children count the objects aloud and match the objects to the corresponding number. Finally, the children color the items freely.

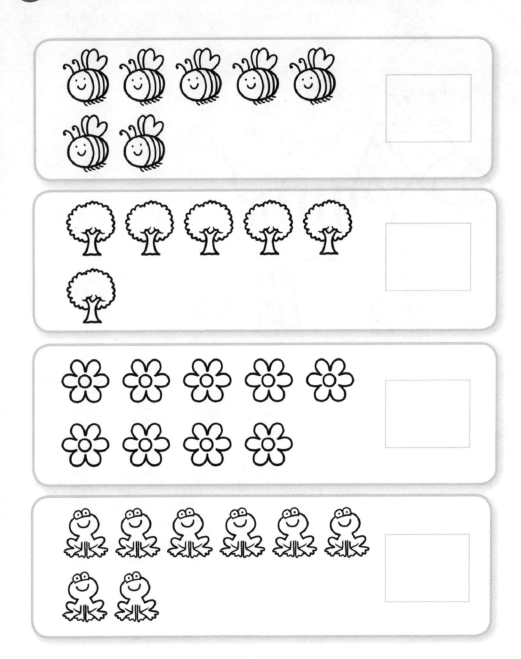

7

8

9

10

1 **Finger-paint. Trace and write.**

Present the letter. The children dip their fingers in finger paint and print their fingerprints along the letter "z" and the zebra. Then the children trace and write the letters with different colored crayons.

Z Z Z Z Z Z Z Z Z Z Z

Z

1 **Count and color the pictures. Trace.**

Review the numbers from 1 to 15. Then the children count the objects in each box and trace the corresponding number. Finally, the children color the pictures freely.

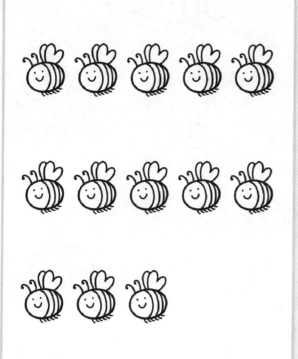

1 **Trace the letters. Color the pictures.**

The children trace the letters with different colored crayons. Then the children color the objects freely.

a b c d e

f g h i j k

l m n o p

q r s t u

v x y z

1 **Count and trace the numbers.**

The children count the lily pads aloud. Next, they trace the numbers.

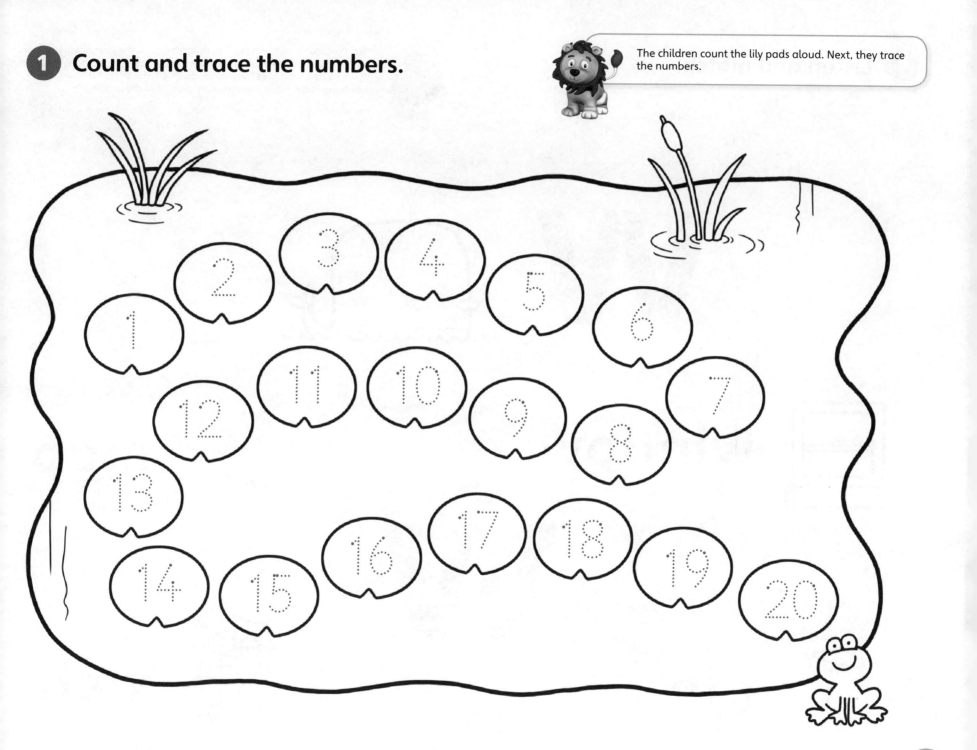

1 **Listen and match.**

Say *Point to the wet whale.* The children follow the instructions. Say /w/ – /w/ – /w/ – *wet.* The children copy. Say /w/ – *window, is it the same sound? Yes!* Match window with the letter "w". Continue in the same manner with the rest of the activity.

 <u>w</u>indow

 <u>m</u>ap

W

 <u>p</u>in

 <u>w</u>eb

1 Make a bee.

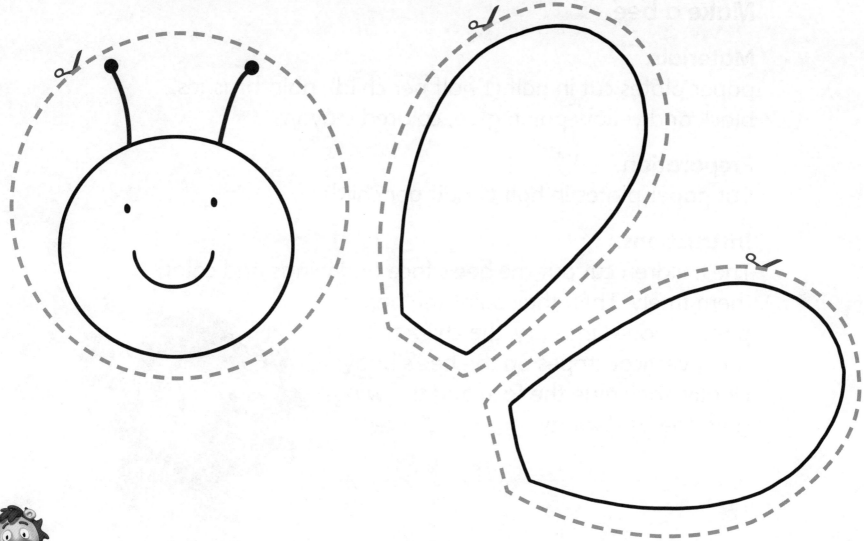

Make a bee.

Materials:
paper plates cut in half (1 half per child), paintbrushes, black and yellow paint, glue, colored crayons

Preparation:
Cut paper plates in half (1 half per child).

Instructions:
The children cut out the bee's face and wings and color them freely. Then they paint the paper plate yellow. Once dry, the children paint vertical stripes on the bee's body. Finally, they glue the face and the wings onto the bee's body.

1 Look and match.

Say *Point to the big spider*. The children follow the instruction. Continue in the same manner with the rest of items on the page. Then show the children how to match the big items with the small items using crayons.

Thanks and acknowledgements

The publishers are grateful to the following contributors:

Blooberry Design: cover design, book design, publishing management and page make-up
Bill Bolton: cover illustration

The publishers and authors are grateful to the following illustrators:

Bill Bolton 1, (1 and repeats on all pages of Leo); Louise Gardner 10, 13, 21, 23, 27, 33, 37, 39, 41, 43, 45, 46, 49, 57, 59, 61, 63, 65, 67, 71, 73, 76, 77, 81, 85, 87, 89, 91, 93, 95; Marek Jagucki 4, 19, 20, 25, 29, 31, 35, 40, 47, 51, 55, 60, 68, 69, 75, 79, 83, 95; Bernice Lum 5, 6, 7, 8, 9, 11, 12, 13, 15, 16, 18, 22, 26, 28, 30, 32, 36, 38, 42, 48, 50, 56, 58, 62, 66, 70, 72, 76, 78, 80, 82, 86, 88, 90, 92